Spur of the Moment

THE WESTERN CARTOON ART OF BEN CRANE

FORWARD BY BOOTS REYNOLDS   TEXT BY PHIL CALLAWAY

While you're looking at the paintings in this book, keep an eye out for a hidden spur in each piece. A mild brain-fart in 1994 caused this eccentricity to begin and I've been doing it ever since. At the back of the book there is a key to all the spur locations from these paintings but don't go cheating and check there before you lose your hair first.

As well, several of these paintings are available as reproductions. You can find a comprehensive list of these at www.bencrane.com as well as how to contact me regarding commissions or other forms of losing your money to me. - Ben

Enjoy the work you see here but don't even think of copying or reproducing any part of this book in any way, shape or form without first securing Ben Crane's permission in writing. Or we'll have to send Mongo, and he hasn't eaten for 3 weeks now . . .

ISBN 0-9695300-5-6

Published in Canada by
Spur of the Moment
Division of Spur Graphics
RR4, Eckville, Alberta T0M 0X0
Phone: 403-729-2747
Fax: 403-729-2746
Email: ben@bencrane.com
Website: www.bencrane.com

Distributed by:
Nevajo Ranch
22556 Township Road 515A
Sherwood Park, Alberta T8A 1H5
Canada
Phone: 780-467-8900
Email: nevajo@planet.eon.net

DEDICATION

For my loving wife, Sharmon, my Nancy Russell, who somehow understands the heart of an artist, and for
Steph and Jessica, who are convinced their daddy is the best artist in the whole world, and for Mom and
Dad, who never once discouraged me from any aspect of art as a hobby or career - this is all your fault!
and for Cordell, my mentor - you're smiling now, old friend.

FORWARD

My secatery steped in the door of my studio and sead,

"There's a guy on the phone from Canada sase he's Been Crane...wonts you to write a forward to a new book he's doing..."

"I didn't know Been could write."

"No...no...it's a book of his pantings."

"Oh. Well I know about that. Let me tell yea about the first time I met Ben..."

"Make it short - I'm on hold here."

"Ok, ok. It's in Cody Wyoming at the first ever cowboy cartoonist meeting. I remember couse the mayor of Cody was giving a welkomning speach when Dr. Miller stude up and anouced that Buffalo Bill was gay. And Ben let out that cackling giggle. That's when I first noticed Ben...in fact every one noticed Ben, espacilly the Mayor's wife, who was setting next to him. I don't think she'll ever get those stanes out of that dress..."

"Ok, ok; but what about his work - his art, his cartooning...what about the book?"

"Oh, that. Well of course he's good; one of the best. Not only can he paint, he knows what he's panting, and tells a good story with a brush or a song. And it didn't hert that he married well eather."

"So you wont me to tell him you'll write the forward?"

"Of course. Just tell him to make the check out to cash!"

Boots Reynolds
Idaho, 2002

– Phil Callaway

It is said that genius is one step away from a lot of things. Insanity being one of them. And it makes perfect sense when you meet Ben Crane. Years ago, when the Creator was handing out gifts, He blessed Ben with a contagious laugh and a twisted wit that make you wonder if the boy could use a good psychiatrist. But when Ben picks up a paintbrush, the psychiatrist is long forgotten. Talent oozes from his fingertips and onto the canvas. A smile tugs at the corners of his mouth as the characters come to life.

This guy may be crazy, but genius can afford to be.

Rumors abound about the origins of cowboy cartoonist Ben Crane. Some say he was born on a boat while his parents escaped from Alcatraz, and that he began doodling immediately. Others believe he is the result of a horrible experiment gone wrong. An experiment in which scientists tried to pool the genes of Norman Rockwell and Bart Simpson. But Ben's mother insists he was born the normal way on May 1, 1963 in Elmira, New York, the third child of Anna and Howie Crane.

"He was a content and happy baby," recalls his mother. "His biggest pleasure was making others laugh." Ben did this in a variety of ways, most of them disgusting. His antics continue to this day. "The wind at his back was usually his own," jokes a friend. "Still is, for that matter."

Moving west in August of 1965, the Cranes planned to settle on a ranch somewhere near Wyoming, but took a right and kept going until the wheels fell off their oxcart in the small town of Three Hills, Alberta, Canada.

Born with a webbed left hand, it was clear that Ben would never play a mandolin,

Ben with Jack & Dena Davis

excel at sports, or make a living with his hands. But the Creator had other ideas. An operation to separate the fingers was performed, but not before two-year-old Ben picked up some crayons and surprised everyone by drawing cartoon characters and creating his own illustrated books. He even gave himself a pen name: Fred MacKenzie. In church one Sunday (while taking careful sermon notes of course) "Fred" began putting shadows on his illustrations. He was only four.

Howie and Anna strongly encouraged Ben's interest in art. They never belittled his doodlings, just asked him to scrub them off the wall. "Ben was a noisy and hyperactive child," says Anna. "Often to get him to take a nap I put an arm and a leg over him until he fell asleep. Yet he could sit quietly for hours copying every little detail of a steam locomotive from the encyclopedia. He was observant and found humor in almost everything." Ben also developed a love for western music that would later be reflected on three popular albums.

School didn't come as easily for Ben though. His math, science, and social studies marks began slipping in first grade. So rather than read books, he drew pictures in the upper right-hand corners of the pages so that classmates who fanned their way through enjoyed live-action cartoons for free. His teachers were not impressed. But his mother was. She hired Brian Parlane, a local artist and head of the Art Department at Prairie Bible Institute, to tutor Ben and his younger sister Carrie. "As they peeked over the edge of the table," remembers Brian, "I tried to help them gain perspective, discover shapes and textures, and use different mediums."

Life did not always reflect art in those days. Much time was left over for mischief with childhood buddies and helping in his father Howie's machine shop.

On a warm spring day in 1978, as Ben swept the floor, Brian Parlane came in to ask if he would be interested in apprenticing as an artist. Ben gazed at the broom for less than a second and knew the answer.

History does not record whether the shop's floors were finished that day, just that the young artist, at age 14, never again picked up a broom (just ask his wife).

Age 11

For nearly a decade Ben continued to wilt in school, but bloom under Brian's quiet, gentle tutorage. His talents were also shaped by two other Art Directors, Phil Callaway and Paul Steinhauer whom Ben credits with helping him develop the character needed to produce a well-rounded illustrator. "Ben has always had an integrity mixed with honor and seasoned by wit, grit and a dash of natural human mischief," says Paul Steinhauer. "What I like about Ben Crane's art is that, no matter which way the wind blows, the laughter comes from the belly, uncontrived and true to life. If horses wore crowns Ben would be one!"

Age 14

Though Ben has yet to wear a crown, he loves horses. When not getting bucked off one or chasing others around the bush country in Alberta's Rockies, he began to soak up the talents of numerous artists. A dry, British sort of goofiness had long ago invaded the Crane household, and Ben's Grandma "Bea," along with her distinguished cat Amy Coffeetea, kept three volumes of Walt Kelly's *Pogo*, whose wit complimented the southern humor his parents and grandmother Bea had imported from the States. During French class in tenth grade, his instructor introduced him to Goscinny and Uderzo's Asterix series. Ben never did learn to read a word of French, but he loved the pictures and later sought out English copies. Jack Davis, one of the founding fathers of *Mad* magazine, also left his fingerprints on Ben, and in 1993 he finally got to meet the man, or as Ben insists, Jack got to meet him.

While chauffeuring Jack around Las Vegas, Ben shot questions at him relentlessly and from close range. Questions like, "What brand of ink do you use?" "What exact brush?" "How in the world do you get the lines to stop shaking when your hand won't cooperate?" and "Can fat people go skinny dipping?" The perfect southern gentleman, Jack took them all in stride. Neither Ben nor Jack knew their friendship would continue through the years.

Age 16

A rare glimpse into realism; this piece was done while I was at Prairie, for an article about a kid whose crime landed him before the law. The judge threw the book at him, then took off his robe and stood beside the boy to pay his penalty for him. Turned out that the judge was the boy's daddy. Graphically illustrates what God did for you and me. ▶

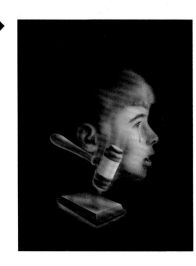

Ben with Boots Reynolds

"I'm so thankful for all the friends I've managed to pick up along the way," says Ben. "They've helped me far more than I've helped them." Alberta ranchers Don and Colleen Wudel, are two such friends. "Some people are unusual," laughs Don, "but indescribable. A long trip in a small car with Ben will bring a tear to your eye for more than one reason! Best of all, Ben's greatest love is for God, then for his wife and the girls. His talents are God's gifts to a serious world. We thank Ben for sharing them with us, they make us laugh."

"We were impressed with Ben's cartoon art from first sight and knew this was one talented teenager," agree Alberta saddle-makers Chuck and Heather Stormes. "Both his technique and sense of humor seemed too sophisticated to belong to a kid. It's been fun for us to track the progress of Ben's career and remember those early drawings that so clearly showed both his artistic talent and his outrageous sense of humor."

Any great artist is only as good as the ideas within, and Ben readily admits that he has shamelessly "borrowed" a few from some great sources through the years: like the fine cartoonists who paint for Leanin' Tree, the greeting card company loved throughout the world for its western humor. He especially credits Mike Scovel, Boots Reynolds, Bonnie Shields and Nate Owens. When they extended Ben an invitation to show his work with them and join a Starving Cartoonists Support Group, Ben jumped at the opportunity. By the time the show was over, the Cowboy Cartoonists International (CCI) was born. Ben was included with the famous 12 Founding Members, along with Wendy Liddle, Zella Strickland, Chris Hammack, Mad Jack "Jock" Hanks, Doc Miller, Bud McCaulley and Paul Crites. Poor Cody, Wyoming may never recover from some of the shenanigans that went on in their fair town. Just ask the Mayor. And the prison guards.

While Ben served as President of CCI for 4 years, from 1996 to 2000, folks from all over became avid collectors of his work. "My wife Linda and I were instantly drawn to Ben's art," writes Malcolm Anderson, an early collector from Jasper, Alberta. "The plain truth was that I loved what I saw and knew that others, who were much more knowledgeable on the cowboy side of life would love it too. The piece with the roped calf running under the horse at the branding fire always brings a smile to both of us, no matter how tough things are."

"I'll never forget the first time I saw some of Ben's art work," jokes Bonnie Shields, the famed Tennessee mule artist, "How it got on the wall in the ladies room, I'll never know." Then she gets serious. "Ben's work is easy to spot and his style is quite distinctive. I was drawn to the clarity of his lines and the purity of his colors. Ben's art is authentic. You can feel the pain and taste the dirt of Alberta in every line. Ben peoples our world with grins."

Mike Scovel, a Texan, and Leanin' Tree's highest-selling artist shares those sentiments. "The first time I met Ace Reid and Jack Davis I told them how pleased I was to meet them and how I had enjoyed their work ever since I was a little kid," says Mike. "I had no idea how devastating those words were until Ben Crane sauntered up to me at an art show in Cody, Wyoming. He introduced himself and said, pretty much, those same words but he used 'young pup', His Sweet 'n, Sour day is sneakin' up on him though. When it does I hope he smiles and swallers hard."

Behind every great man is an amazed woman. And behind every great cowboy cartoonist is a great encourager. One who believes that if the show will ever be a success, he'd better aim the spotlight at the stage. "I'm convinced I wouldn't be doing this if it weren't for the encouragement of Boots Reynolds," says Ben, who is quick to call Boots one of his most important mentors. "Several times over my career he took me aside, completely unsolicited, and encouraged the hang out of me." Boots always started out by telling Ben what he was doing right and that served as a doorway to other positive suggestions as to how he could tweak things to be even more successful. Today, Boots is regarded as the grandfather of cowboy cartoonists and is dearly loved and looked up to by so many. "Boots has risen so high because he pulls others up with him," explains Ben. "He just plain encourages folks and seeks to bring out the best in other artists. He doesn't hold his cards to his vest like so many. Instead, he lets folks in on the secrets of his success. He truly wants success for others. This has been a real source of encouragement for me as an artist."

©Mike Scovel. Used by permission

Portrait of Ben by Mike Scovel

In June of 1990, Ben swallowed hard and sported a wide grin as he carried his new bride Sharmon over the threshold of their little rental house in the Canadian Rockies. "There was no money in the bank and no food in the cupboard," recalls Ben, "and a man cannot live on adoration alone, so against Sharm's advice, I bought a computer system for layout and design." Enough jobs came in to make the monthly installments, but he decided never again to make a major decision without his wife's consultation.

"She's my Mary Russell," Ben says of Sharm, recalling that it was only after Charlie Russell's wife got involved with his art that he was able to turn it into an income. "I got brains only for drawing, making music, and making rude noises. She's got the brains for business." Ben credits Sharm for any successes he's had in the art world because she can somehow see past the personal attachment he has to his work. She has also helped him see that an artist can work regular hours and leave the evenings and weekends open for family and recreation. "If I hit a project completely rested," says Ben, "my work is far better."

One day on a trip west of Sundre, Alberta, Brian Parlane and Ben ended up at the Helmer Creek Ranch. Had Brian understood what he was about to unleash upon the world, he may have headed for home, but instead he introduced Ben to one of Canada's foremost cowboy poets, Bryn Thiessen, and the two became close friends. Both share the same warped sense of humor, and to this day they can get into more trouble than a skunk in a balloon factory. It is not uncommon for them to wrangle their way out of a coffee shop or Vietnamese restaurant tab with an original ink drawing and accompanying poem.

Many of the pieces you see in this book are the result of these two twisted minds at work–though Ben insists he hasn't worked a day in his life since dropping that broom in the spring of '78. "If you would have told me years ago that I'd make a handsome living doing the thing that got me in trouble throughout school," he laughs, "I'd have checked your temperature and bought you some aspirin."

Although at first their work seems senselessly silly, when studied over time, it gets worse. I'm kidding of course. At the very least, Ben's work records western life laid bare. "Historically, humor has been one of the strongest fibers holding together a culture shaped by hard work and hard times," says Ben, offering a rare glimpse at his philosophical side. "Besides, life is hilarious. I can't keep a straight face when I look in the mirror so how can I keep one when I see a cow with her tongue up her nose? This world is fearfully and wonderfully weird."

According to some, Ben's art reflects a bit of a self-portrait. "I consider myself somewhat refined," laughs Jane Trumble, Vice President of Product Development for Leanin' Tree in Boulder, Colorado, "but it's tough to be when you publish the artwork of Ben Crane on our western humor cards."

▲ **Hardening Of The Arteries;** Ben's first bronze sculpture.

In the early days of going to CCI shows and meetings, Jane had the "pleasure" of being seated next to Ben during dinner. She very soon realized she was sitting next to Emily Post's worst nightmare! "I don't really explicitly recall all the examples of 'bad' manners," she says, "except that somewhere during the meal, between good-natured belches and elbow pokes, Ben actually put a finger in his nose... or made it look like he was putting a finger in his nose. Looked pretty real to me! Ben subtly sprinkles the worst manners with some of the best manners you've ever seen and then he gets you laughing so quickly that you just get swept away. I suppose it's no wonder that one of our best selling cards ever

features a painting of Ben's of a cow with his tongue up his nose. I think Emily would have been publicly horrified, but privately envious of how Ben captivated the crowd that night. And I left feeling as if I had spent an evening sitting next to royalty!"

Not everyone shares Jane's appreciation for that infamous card.

Once at a CCI show in Oklahoma City at the National Cowboy Hall of Fame, he watched a rather dignified mother and her teenager wander into his booth and pick up The Salt Lick Card, which shows a cow spelunking its nasal passages. "They wrinkled their noses in complete disgust," recalls Ben, "and they almost lost their lunch when they opened the card and read: *'Picked this one out especially for you!'*" Looking at Ben with disgust, they stomped out of the booth. Ben pointed at another artist and hollered, "It's his!"

"I suppose rural folk get more out of my work than city folk do," says Ben. His greatest compliments come from those who live the life and say, "You've obviously been there. You can't paint this stuff if you haven't been."

During a story on Ben's work, a CBC reporter asked him where he drew the line in his humor. A self-described "multilingual illiterate," Ben stumbled for an answer, so the reporter came to his aid. "You're saying that you'll do disgusting but you won't do vulgar?" Ben nodded and grinned.

"My value system is based on the Bible I learned at my mother's knee," says Ben, "and it's taken deep root. I think it's much harder to pull good humor from everyday life than to fall back on the dirt and vulgarity that so many do." Then he smiles. "At least I can sleep at night. I would rather let people laugh with a clear conscience and leave them unembarrassed in front of their children."

Asked many times where he gets his inspiration, Ben says simply, "Look around you." Many of the concepts in the pieces he does are the result of unusual situations he finds himself in, or scenes recounted to him by others. Often at art shows, old timers study the paintings and start in on stories of their lives. Ben's overactive imagination fills in the blanks.

In the back of their minds, Ben and Sharm have always longed for a place of their own. So recently they bought seven acres of land near Leslieville, Alberta, and perched their house and studio atop a ridge with the perfect mountain view. To the north lie acres of poplar forest, sections of which have become backgrounds for his paintings. To the west and south the view is glorious, the sunsets stunning. Marble and Limestone Mountains surround old haunts from his childhood, giving Ben the feeling that he's come full circle and now owns the world.

"I reckon I'm home now," he smiles past a weathered moustache.

And he is.

Though his work has been collected across Canada and the States, and as far away as Europe; though the accolades continue to pour in, Ben considers his greatest accomplishments "convincing my wife to keep me and fathering two young 'uns."

Recently Ben's mother handed him two large scrapbooks of work she had saved since his early childhood. "Some of my new stuff is almost as good as these," he jokes.

But not even the laughter of genius can mask Ben's tender heart when he talks about the things that matter most to him. "I'm so blessed to think that people have my work hanging on their walls, and hopefully they will long after I'm gone. I'm glad I can make some people laugh, but more than that I hope I'll be remembered as a good husband and dad. A man of faith and integrity. I guess I just wanna live so the preacher won't have to lie at my funeral!"

And before you know it, the contagious laughter of genius has returned.

▲ In the bush when *Marrianne* was born
with poet and guide Fred Miller

Richard Farnsworth, actor, ▶
with a Ben Crane caricature.

NOBODY EVER SAID IT WAS GONNA BE EASY!

▼ *Close on the heels of the Vaquero, this was the first piece Chuck took into his shop. Somebody related to the overall feel of the piece and took it home.*

▲ **VAQUERO**

This is the piece what started it all; I was 17 at the time and done this up for family friend Len Yule, Kentucky rawhide braider and horse trainer. Len told me that he was intensely interested in the life of the old Spanish vaquero, the ancestor of today's cowboy. This is what might happen if the bull's a little persistent and ain't about to change direction.

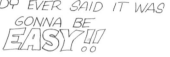

NOBODY EVER SAID IT WAS GONNA BE
EASY!!

▲ TOO LATE TO DUCK

Anybody what's rode in the bush will have a personal understanding of this feller's plight. Their foresight will probably have increased dramatically by the next time they went out. Ask Bryn about his close encounters with the odd spruce tree; he come back the other day with a bloodied-up face on account of the fight he had. The tree won.

UNCONTROLLED CROSSING ▶

I've always been fascinated by the southwestern desert, and my mind went to wandering as to what might make a good wreck down there. Momma roadrunner seems right put out that somebody might be jaywalking in front of her fambly. I wonder where the rider ended up.

▲ JUVENILE DELINQUENT

If calves are anything like other kids, this is what happens when momma calls. That's her down below, bawling for junior. He got a different kind of bawling when he gave up his hiding place and went home for supper.

◀ THAT'LL DO

Another dizzy picture. A loose stock dog has a tendency to work all the time and most often tends to lend his help when it ain't called for. Makes for an interesting day when you're laying on some schooling to a green horse.

That'll Do!

I had not really worked on lighting up until this point, and it took me quite by surprise that this piece actually looked to me like it was taking place outside. Looking back at that time I realized that my pieces looked like they were all under overcast skies. I started taking a look at contrast between the shadows and the highlights, and then as I painted more, I started concentrating on where the shadow of each object might fall over other objects. This lighting never really took effect until probably '94.

CAST IRON COCINERO

Cocinero is Spanish for cook. The model for this is an old friend, Rick Plett. His cooking reminded me of this scene. I try not to show up at his place around mealtime when his wife ain't home.

SEEING EYE TO EYE

Why is it that the smallest guys always pick the highest horses and the tallest fellers usually ride the shortest? It all evens out in the end though.

SECOND BEST

One of those things kids might do to make do when the real thing ain't around. Kids have the best imaginations - not reined in and suppressed like most respectable adults. And who has the most fun?

◄ UPCHUCK

Sharm gave the incredible name to this piece. I had watched a documentary on the Cochrane Hooves Of History cattle drive. On the tape was some good footage of a runaway with a wagon and I got to thinking about what would happen if a feller too late discovered that the ford he always took every spring was washed out.

Exaggeration

*This was the first time I loosened up and added a good exaggerated expression on folks' faces. Up until then my most common facial expression had simply been surprise - wide open eyes. I finally woke up and started adding other expressions like laughter, anger, pain, intensity. I'd been pretty mellow in my portrayal of life, and that isn't very consistent with cartooning. Even the build of my animals was incredibly conservative. BORING. Finally by **They Went Thataway** I had skinnied up the necks, enlarged the heads a bit, and pretty well introduced the style that I've maintained and tweaked over the years to become my own.*

◀ **MIDWIFE CRISIS**

Originally the cover for one of Betty Kilgour's Crocus Coulee series of books, this seems to appeal to the ranch wives for some reason. I don't think the husband is in a heated cab, so don't get too worked up!

On a Roll

Near the end of 1991, I added what was to become my trademark—that evasive little spur hidden in every piece. On a piece called "When Long Days Get Longer," I hid some toilet paper, or what my brother-in-law Jesse Lynch calls an after-dinner roll, and a spur in the foreground. Although I really liked the idea of the toilet paper, I reckon I had to stick with the spur on account of the name of my business; Spur-Of-The-Moment.

▲ **CORRAL #9**   *For years my brother Matt told me this was really what the name of this famous perfume was. Being he was much older and much wiser I naturally believed him.*

ONCE A YEAR ▶

Sharm came up with this idea. The original version was the tall skinny one, and Leanin' Tree asked if I might redo it in a format that would fit with their cards, so I done it with a few major changes so the two collectors wouldn't go to war over who had the real original. This is about as indecent as some fellers I know would dare get. And about as clean; I think he's scrubbing with an old piece of chaw. That'll strip the paint. The second version was named by Don Wudel who has a much better grasp of wordsmithing than do I. He calls it What I Can't Soak Off I Can Chip.

▲ A RUDE AWAKENING

There's a habit I've got - seeing human characteristics in animals. I'm sure this happened somewhere.

◀ SALT LICK I & II

The story behind this piece is wrote in the text (p.10). This is one piece where there is no middle ground; folks either love it or hate it. They tell me a good piece of art will draw a reaction from the observer. I didn't know it could draw blood! The original version, black and white, was inked in '92; colour version followed the next year.

PREMEDITATED MANOUVRE

Here I go again on human character in animals. Bryn and Sharm and I were out joyriding on the Helmer one day when we come across this deadfall. Jumping contests soon ensued and I reckon Bryn won on account of he jumped and ducked at the same time. Of course the split was a foot higher in real life but I thought this might make a better story.

▲ SITTIN' DOWN ON THE JOB

This was our little place on the James River. I never been much of a farrier, but I seen horses do this to the best of them; Nathan, Murray & Dale - here's to you!

▼ BEAR NECESSITIES

Another dull day at the laundromat. I reckon it'll be after dark before this boy gets back to camp tonight. You can see that spruce needles ain't the only pokeys he's going to encounter while he's assessing this new view of the world.

▲ ICHABOD

We've all seen this guy in our neighbor's pasture. Leanin' Tree has used this feller on mugs and t-shirts as well as cards, with the slogan "Are you SURE you want to be the next person to get on my nerves?"

▼ THERE'S ONE IN EVERY CROWD

This happened to Jim Neufeld one day while they were sorting. Nearly killed him, but a year after the wreck I asked if he'd mind if I put this down. That's really me in the foreground I think; I'm the idiot who often sees the funny side of a bad wreck. Unless it happens to me of course.

Self-portraits

In order to laugh at somebody else I realized I had to laugh at myself first. These are some of the buffetings I gave myself over the years. You can tell I'm right flattering to myself as well as everybody else I paint.

▲ DAISY & DANDELIONS FOR DAISY

Peggy Copithorne will never pose for me again. I just took the liberty to remove a few of her teeth and purty her up a bit... Rick Plett wormed his way into this piece too. This is what I've always imagined older courtship to look like. The dogs seem to know more of what's happening than the people do.

AMOUROUS AUTUMN ▲

This actually happened to my cousin Lyle Pattison and was too good of a story to pass up. Took him quite awhile to sneak his way from bale to bale and escape. I reckon he's too good with the elk call.

Mixed Medium

Other mediums have always interested me, as have mixed mediums, where you use more than one type of pigment to execute your work. Watercolour has never been a good medium to layer thick, heavy, solid colours. So when you come to shadow details you need to find something that can allow you to layer over top of the darks. Coloured pencil did that trick for me - only because that's the only other thing I had in the studio. Not having gone through art school I've not been taught all the tricks and shortcuts and have had to rely on what's hanging around the house. I discovered that the colour pencil sat on top of the paper nicely; the dried watercolour giving almost the texture of a fine sandpaper which held the pencil very well. Besides, my big set of pencils had a real nice purple that I like to use for shadow details; surfaces that reflect light into the dark areas like light reflected of the grass onto a cow's belly.

◀ RIDIN' DRAG

Dale Fehr and I were checking cows on a big pasture in the Sand Hills country of Saskatchewan. This is several stories conglomerated into one, but centred mainly on one cow that would ram him every chance it could while she was on the end of his twine. I just carried it to its logical conclusion and played with the words a bit.

The PRAIRIE BREEZE

The GRASS IS ALWAYS GREENER...

COWLISTHENICS

BOTTOMS UP!

◀ COWLISTHENICS SERIES

This is a series I did based around various positions cows get themselves into. Such a huge beast balancing daintily on three points is beyond me. Ever tried scratching behind your ear with a hind foot? Credit goes to Bryn for the methane-induced haze of the Prairie Breeze, a little poke at the folks what thinks the ozone layer is gone hollow because cows fart (what happens to the air when those folks do?). The idea that the grass is always greener on the other side of the fence don't just apply to cows - that's a human flaw too. And Bottoms Up - you've all seen the calf that was impatient when the tap wasn't flowing fast enough.

BULLSEYE ▶

This is to all the guys that think they're God's gift to women. Translated into bovine I guess you could say she caught his eye when he come calling.

Cowboy Trappings
© 1996 Bryn Thiessen. Used by permission.

I always tip my hat to the ladies,
But this time I got in a wreck.
See, I forgot about this tornado twine
I had around my neck.
It stretched my nape right proper
So in the future what I'll do
Is smile and nod,
And mumble a howdy-do.

COWBOY TRAPPINGS ▶

Bryn and I were wasting time at a pizza joint in Trochu one time, cogitating on what would happen if a feller tried to be respectable when he forgot about his tornado twine. Bryn's poem explains it all. By the way that's me and my wife's grandmother, Ruth Pattison.

New Tools

This is the first time I used a brush for inking. I loved the result - this was a larger piece and the only brush I had that was the right shape was pretty big and it wouldn't work for finer lines. So I went back to the frustrating quill nib until One Cheek Sneak, where I had just returned from Vegas and a week with Jack Davis, who had told me what brush to use. I use a Windsor-Newton Series 7 Number 3, fine sable. With practice I found I can get pretty well any thickness from about a half-inch down to a hair line. I finally found a way to have a freedom in my lines that I couldn't get with a quill nib.

I SAID HEEL!

The scene is the calving pen here on the home place. Here's to all who have waterskiied behind a first-calf heifer whose labour pangs was interrupted by the help of a dog who took the heel command a little too literally. Sometimes I think that when somebody says they got a good stock dog they're probably lying.

IN YOUR DREAMS! ▶

Rob Holland tells me of the time he and another feller took a pack trip from Grande Prairie down to Sundre through the back country. They came to this muskeg, his saddle horse steps through quietly, and his first pack mule jumps. His feet goes out from beneath him and he goes under clear to the tips of his ears and the top of his pack. When he stands up he's pitch black, then he opens his eyes. That's when the boys lost it, and couldn't get back in the saddle for a half hour on account of their hurting sides. The title reflects the last mule's mental state.

◀ ITCHIN' FOR A BRITCHIN'

This is my all-time favourite piece. Fred Miller and I were guiding German and Dutch tourists in the Clearwater country near Harrison Flats, when we decided one day to spice up the trip with rides on greenbroke mules. Going up to the Elk Flats wasn't bad, but coming down was a different story, with no britching to hold the saddle in place. Didn't help that they was built somewhat like an oil barrel either. I adjusted my saddle three times on the way down and this is what I felt like. That was my first and last ride on a mule; Fred's swore off horses and rides only mules. You draw your own conclusions.

▼ WATCHA DOIN' GRAMPA

Lyle and Karan Gleddie tell this story of one of their daughters at a branding.
Kids always seem to ask the best questions at the best times and for once
Grampa didn't have nothing to say.

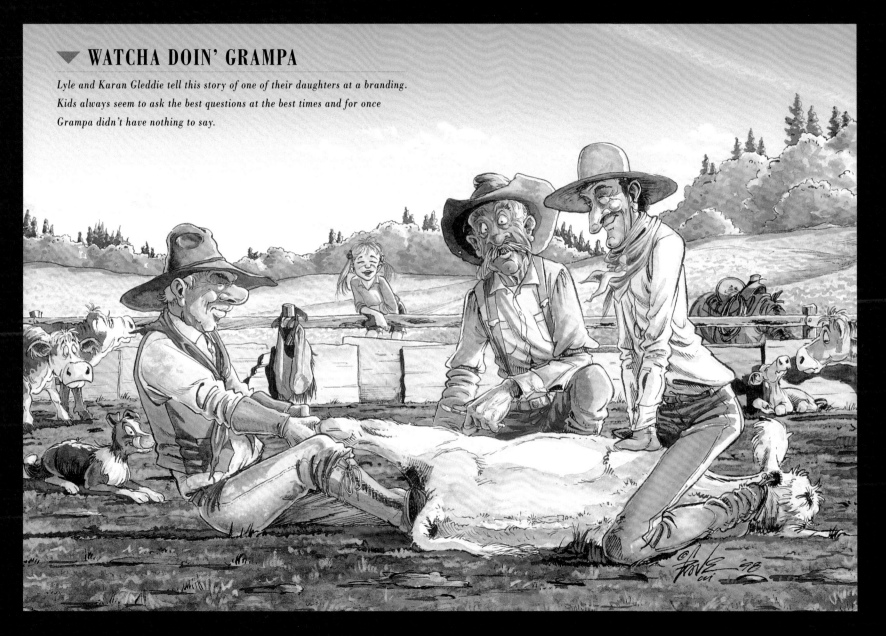

HEARD YOU WAS LOOKING FOR A HAND ▶

This is the culture clash where the new city guy comes out to lend a hand for a gather. He's trying to help but don't realize he's astride the wrong form of transportation. Quads and stock don't mix all that well. Nor does quads and cowboys.

▲ AND YOU THOUGHT YOUR TROUBLES WERE BEHIND YOU

Art Thompson tells me a true story about a feller who was packing in supplies for his camp up by the Yukon. Seems the hemmorhoids was acting up something fierce and this feller slides off to do some doctoring, and when he was incapacitated out pops momma griz looking for junior who just happened to be on the other side of Mr. Piles. Seems momma was too surprised at the view to take offensive action and he was able to hobble back to his saddle horse, although he had to ride five or six miles back down the trail to retrieve his pack string and most of the grub.

◀ THAT SINKING FEELING

Sharm and I were watching a cow mucking around in the muskeg cooling her feet and chomping down her salad, when my mind started wandering again. I have no idea how it got from there to here, other than wondering how big a splash she might make if she jumped in. I love the perspective in this piece; not often do you see a horse from this angle.

ICE CAPADES

Kurt Browning was in the news for another one of his wins when Bryn and I start putting his lifestyle together with that of his dad Dewey, a feller what knows horses, trails and the bush country. This is what come out the other end.

▲ I TRAINED HIM MYSELF

This was a true story too although it took place outside and I have to refrain from naming the folks what saw it on account of the witness protection program. So we'll just blame the scene on the man who hasn't learned to put the seat down yet, even after 40 years of wedded bliss.

▲ HE WAS JUST A HUNDRED YARDS FROM MARIANNE

Fred Miller and I were wondering what would happen if your pack string decided to pass you on a double line. Seems that the wreck always happens at the very end of your trip, hence the title. Better duck because that owl's going to land in your lap in a minute.

▼ CAFE OLÉ

One of those plays on a phrase. This feller's been in the saddle all day staring at the back end of a cow, and the coffee smells mighty inviting even if there is no cream. One of the herd bulls mistakes his shaking the rain out of his slicker and you can fill in the rest of the wreck.

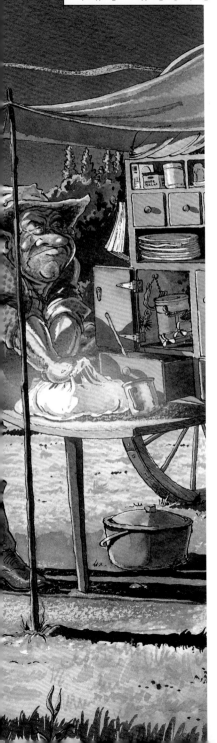

Real Life

The haunts near home provide much of my backgrounds and subject matter. My time spent in the bush hunting, camping and fishing with my family gives authenticity to the background detail; the way deadfall lays scattered like matchsticks in "In Your Dreams," or the muskeg willows and humpgrass beckon in "He Was Just A Hundred Yards From Marianne." Actual places are represented as well. "Cafe Olé" is on the flats near Barrier Mountain heading out to Alberta's Ya Ha Tinda, the Canadian government ranch that raises horses for the federal parks. "Return Of The Redeye" showcases Bryn's Helmer Creek Ranch southwest of Sundre. "Grateful, Ain't She?" is from the southwest quarter of the home section of Sharm's family, a mile west of my house, and the background of "The Back Nine" is the view out of the north window of my studio.

ONE CHEEK SNEAK ▲

Chivalry on the trail ain't all it's cracked up to be. This boy tried to let one sort of seep out but there was more pressure there than he had planned. The gal is being right hospitable though, pretending not to notice. The dog and the mice are a little more honest however.

▲ BODACIOUS BOVINE BABES

Ever notice the wide variety of hair styles in any given herd? I've seen every one of these gals on the homeplace here except the last one - I wondered what she'd look like with all her hair slipped on account of her age. The lovely Miz Doris Used-To-Be-Daley come up with some fantastic individual titles for these babes for a trade of a cast-iron skillet. I'm not recollecting whether I made good on the trade yet.

Brighten Up

Perhaps the most significant signature of my style is the intensity of the color. Many folks don't believe that I use watercolor because of the brightness of my work, but neither can they pin down the medium that would act that way. I simply use a lot of pigment with very little water. It's essential to use good quality paints and transparent colors to let my ink work show through. I'm not afraid to let the paper show through to create the brilliant whites of the highlights created by the sun. High contrast between the highlights and shadows also enhances the impression of a hot sun at midday on "Turnabout Is Fair Play," or the low sun of "He Was Just A Hundred Miles From Marianne" or the brightly moonlit night scene of "Zelda, Queen Of The Herd."

WHAT A STUPID-LOOKING HAT ▶

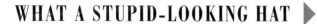

Fred Miller and Stan Radke tell of the time when a German tourist gal shows up to their camp a little less than congenial. Seems that this is one of the first things she says after dismounting and taking a good look from Stan's toe to his head. Best part of the story is that this is pretty much exactly what she looked like.

▲ ZELDA - QUEEN OF THE HERD

Late nights and strong coffee do wonders when they're mixed with the brains of Bryn and myself, complicated by the fact that we needed a Christmas scene for the calendar and we only had three days before it goes to press. I have no idea where the giraffe came from. But everyone understands mistletoe.

▼ RETURN OF THE REDEYE

This is a common scene with range cows. One eye's always got to be peeled for momma who is convinced you're trying to kill her baby. This is what Bryn looks like from behind. Funny thing is, you can recognize him from this side!

GRATEFUL, AIN'T SHE?

Alan Donelly commissioned this piece from me, a story from a book he was reading. Seems momma just couldn't express her heartfelt appreciation in a way that the feller with the shovel could really relate to. The Alberta mosquito coming in for a landing would later reappear in a series of its own.

A GOOD BRAND OF TRAILMIX ▶

This idea came from Rob Holland, who understands the meaning of trailmix. I sorter like the toilet paper, soaring in a graceful arc over the whole scene. The look on the old boy's face says he's been there before.

Bees Mr. Bees

*This outhouse would become the distraught scene of one of my better-known pieces, "**Bees In The Outhouse**," which I also turned into a song nominated in 2000 for the Academy of Western Artists (AWA) Will Rogers Memorial Award in the humorous poetry category.*

▲ BEES IN THE OUTHOUSE

A more intimate look into the personal life of Ben Crane. This happened to me in 1989 at my place on the James. Had to change the identity to protect the innocent. I looked for the nest after I calmed down and found it brazenly planted between the two holes, not 6" from the latter part of my unsuspecting anatomy. I have no idea how long that nest must have been there, but it must of been awhile because it was a good 6" across. How I escaped real injury I'll never know.

Bees In The Outhouse

©1999 Ben Crane, Jinglebob Music (SOCAN / BMI)
From the album When Cowboys Rode As Kings

It's just a simple small two-holer,
Nothing fancy or debonair,
And despite the rough surroundings
All the comfort in the world is there.
'Twas a place I loved to sit and think,
Passing more than just the time,
'Til I discovered that the occupation
Wasn't exclusively mine.

While I was out with the wagon
For the roundup in the spring,
My little house found a new tenant whose
Principle preambulation was wing.
As I sat one day in quiet repose,
My pants down around my knees,
I was startled from my leisure to
A profusion of anxieties.

Chorus
Bees in the outhouse -
A dangerous sort of mix;
If you,re both there at the same time
You're bound to get in a fix.
There's a certain lack of dignity
When you're ambushed from behind,
But I think that they can only sting one time.

So I forgot what urge had sent me there,
All ambition had been denied
Because some little winged varmint and his
Friends made a grown man cry.
They say most vagrants sneak into
The loo to get a buzz,
But it ain't what it's what it's cracked up to be
Out where I live, because of those

Chorus

Bridge
They say one sting will kill them,
And I really hope it's true,
Cause I don't think they deserve to live, do you?

Chorus

▲ **TURNABOUT IS FAIR PLAY**

One of those in-your-face experiences. Some people ask why would a feller rope an animal in that kind of a setting, but you can ask Julian Tubb. He's been there. But then again he lost a finger from roping - and he was on foot when it happened. I like the intense lighting in this piece. This boy ain't sweating just because it's hot though.

▲ **CHINESE FIRE DRILL**

I did this piece as a result of a personal account of a feller I chanced to meet at a show somewhere, and then found out that Baxter Black also told a similar story. It don't matter where in the world you are - the same wrecks can happen to anybody!

▼ BACK NINE

Inspired by a Zane Grey story I was reading recently about a few hands on a desert ranch playing the pastime of the rich and famous. Got to thinking about that and my mind wandered. I think this is how they do it in Bearberry, which, incidently, was supposed to be the place in the title.

▲ DOES THIS HURT YET?

Originally drawn for a dental recall card company, I was wondering what methods of extraction were used when the only anesthetic was some crooner who'd put anyone out for a week.

◀ **BRAINWORMS**

Jesse Lynch, one of my brothers-in-law, trains horses for a living, and commented to me one time about this particular horse that had this particular condition. Made me wonder - did this particular horse have a particularly light-colored mane...

▼ STRIKE FORCE

Saw a photo of Calgary sportsman writer Kyle McNeilly in this pose. Well, sort of. He was holding up a big fat trout but I think this is what was really happening that day. Seems that them who does the work seldom eats the benefits.

Lunch Crew

*This image started the era where artwork was commissioned for cards by Leanin' Tree. Up until this time I simply pitched them anything I did, hoping for a modest return on my gamble. Other commissions to date are **Who Moved My Car?** (Birthdays do wonders...), **You're Not Just An Old Fart, Chick Magnet** and **Two Old Goats**.*

▲ LUNCH CREW

Jane Trumble asked me if I would "paint a bunch of your cows in a line, doing something". They were introducing their long skinny cards and wanted artwork on the back as well as the front, so I did up a line of cows at the dinner table, remeniscent of friends or co-workers (or is that cow-workers...) at lunch together. Naturally for the back it had to be the back view. And you thought that the red cow on the far right of the front was just being Angus with that expression of hers. Goes to show you that things ain't always as they seems.

▼ KID'S HORSE

A farrier friend and I were talking one time about the acreage horses that he gets to go take care of. These are pets that seldom get rode but have free run of the place pasture-wise and boss-wise; we call them lawn ornaments. Now you can understand his brand. Seems that he didn't need a bucket of water for anything but he sent the kid after it so's he could sorter tune the horse in a bit without a peanut gallery. Horse was fine after that.

▲ **WIDER GATES OR SMALLER COWS**

Sometimes I wonder whether animals get real ripped at others of their species, like humans, and act out those tendencies. I suppose an animal psychologist could tell me stories about these two. Maybe about me too. Forget it.

▲ **RAWHIDE** | *I used to teach western horsemanship and wrangle at a couple kids camps and that's the handle they gave me. This is one possible version of where that name sprung from…*

▶ RIDIN' THE RANGER

Friend Clint Havens tells me about a couple old boys that this very thing happened to. The heifer they were chasing disappeared over the edge of a coulee and stopped as the truck baled over top of her; seemed that she knew exactly what she was doing. I thought it might make a better story of it was a couple instead of two bachelors.

▼ FIRST DAY OF THE MILENNIUM

If Y2K actually happened, this scene would be repeated all over the west country; I'da took my place behind the team. The late Howard Jones, Maple Creek, was the unknowing model in this piece, and grateful appreciation goes to his wife. Apologies to photographer John McQuarrie; I figured this was what was really happening in his photo.

▲ LUCKY

Lyle and Karan Gleddie, rancher friends from the desert country of Alberta, discussed this concept with me over lunch at some swanky cafe in downtown Calgary one day. We kept adding injuries until we decided that the pup was worth her name. Her expression says "Hah- but you should see the other dog!" The original concept was roughed out on a napkin.

▼ JUST WHERE DO I START?

An old family friend once commented to me that he was as undecided as a mosquito in a nudist colony. Of course, that sets me to thinking about how the mosquito sees things, and with a smorgasboard like this before her this poor gal just don't know where to start.

▲ CULTURE CLASH

Seems that wherever cowboys go we tend to clash with other cultures. This is what might could of happened if two boys decided to try one of the extreme sports of the cultural elite. I suppose you could call these two pictures my beach series.

▲ BROKE TO LEAD

Of course, the 80 acres of complete open grass can never be enough room to pull an animal into line. The wreck ALWAYS happens where the bush is the thickest. This come about by the mere term "broke to lead", and my mind wandered. Again.

DUCK!

The boy on the back is the only one who don't know exactly what his friend is yelling. Yet. The background here is no place in particular, although it's very representative of the bush country I've loved ever since I was a pup.

I render my original concepts as pencil roughs on cheap typing paper (is there any such thing anymore?) with a soft pencil; usually a 2B or an HB. I do all my erasing and reworking on that paper so that my watercolour paper doesn't get damaged by excessive erasing. When I'm satisfied with the general concept I turn the paper over and cover the back side with a wide graphite stick and then place the rough over my watercolour paper and trace the outlines, transferring the image with lines that can be erased after inking (carbon paper don't work!). This way I can place it wherever I want, creating the proper balance of positive and negative space - simple design rules. Generally each figure or group of figures is drawn on a separate paper so that precise placement can be easily altered, or, I'll trace one figure and then move the paper slightly and trace the next exactly where I want him.

When things look good I'll pull out the brush and ink the lines, using the pencil rough as a detail guide. I may add a bit of shadow or other details with the ink, but mainly it's the outline and a hint of textures. The brush gives me the ability to adjust the width of the line by adjusting the pressure. Generally the thicker lines will be on the shadow side of the object with the thinner on the leading edge, or edge closest to the light source.

Most of the texture details are left for the paint. After the ink is cured, or dried, for a half hour or so I'll start in on the paint. Being watercolour, the general rules are to start with the lightest colours and work your way to the darker ones. I found that I need to paint the sky first and reference my colour intensities for the rest of the piece to that. This process will take several days on average, and then I'll take the next several days to tweak, often sitting back and staring at the fool piece, looking over every detail and second-guesing whether I done it right or not. Finally I get sick and tired of being so finicky and I pronounce it done. Skies are often rendered with an airbrush and acrylic paint. Liquitex has a real nice blue that is closer to a true sky blue than any other pigment I've found. Clouds and the horizon lines are masked with a masking fluid that can exponentially increase your creativity by exposure to the smell. I think maybe my best work has lots of masking on it.

The watercolour paper is stretched out on a hard, smooth wood surface and taped down all around the four edges. I work on an old drafting board that was handed down from my dad and his dad before him. The sliding straightedge and square comes in real handy because I like to square up the edges with a pencil line first, then tape along those lines. That way my piece is perfectly square and is easier not only for reproduction purposes but also keeps my framer from sending Luigi to my front door in the middle of some dark stormy night to exact revenge for her gradual loss of sanity.

▲ HIGH ON THE HAWG

This was commissioned by a friend for a friend. Jude Peters owns a beautiful red Harley, and here we see her on her way to the local establishment to eat and get gas. I've been to lots of those kinds of cafes. The hawgs of her friends are all parked outside and her real bike is there too.

▲ WHO MOVED MY CAR?

Leanin' Tree commissioned this one for a birthday card which said
"Birthdays do wonders for a person . . . Wonder where my glasses
are? Wonder where my car is? Wonder which birthday this is?"
It must have gone over alright; within the first year of its publication it was
sitting as their #1 best-selling card in Leanin' Tree's overall humour
division, outselling the second-place card by three times.

▼ TAKING A TURN FOR THE NURSE

Started this piece as a work-in-progress at the 2000 Calgary Stampede Western
Art Show. I wasn't going to put a nurse in the picture but then this gal comes
walking by and I had to stick her in. Bryn Thiessen came along and named
the piece most aptly.

EVEN AT OUR AGE WE STILL GOT GREAT-LOOKING CALVES! ▶

One of my partners in crime, the incomparable Doris (Daley) Haysom, pitched me this idea. I think she's looking forward to those golden years when gravity takes hold and body parts take on a whole new look. May she age gracefully.

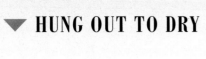

HUNG OUT TO DRY

Sometimes things just get in the way. This piece could also be called "When It's Too Late To Holler".
By the way, horses generally see this shape in their shadow when they need an excuse to blow up.

▲ **SUNFISHER**

This is my attempt to understand that most famous of all bucking styles - the bronc that likes to turn his belly to the sky. It makes for a great show and I have much admiration for an athletic horse. Just looking at it makes my back hurt.

▲ **SEVENTY-THREE SECONDS AND COUNTING**

There's a perverse sense of glee when the skies open up on an outdoor rodeo. The wrecks are more spectacular and you see everything in shades of one colour - dirt. However, you also see more grit; the determination kind, like this feller who just ain't giving up yet even though he's out of the money.

▲ **COLD NOSE**

Another version of an old black-and-white done in '93. I couldn't help thinking what a shock it would be when you were so engrossed in your first taste of new grass after a winter of dry hay that you didn't notice junior coming in for lunch until his cold wet nose hit you from behind.

▲ TWO OLD GOATS

Leanin' Tree commissioned these two pieces in 2001 as a birthday card to an old goat. Ever notice how animals usually tend to look like their owners - or is it the other way around?

This painting was awarded the Western Horseman Magazine Judges' Choice buckle at the 2001 CCI Annual Show.

CHICK MAGNET ▼

They wanted an old feller that was the epitome of animal magnetism - he could still draw flies. Always wanted to paint a piece called the Chick Magnet but for some reason figgered it'd be a caricature of Bryn Thiessen...

RODENTILE DELINQUENT ▼

Always wondered where the gophers go when you're out looking for them. Brad & Kim Devereux, part of my inlaw clan, was hoping to snap up Juvenile Delinquent, but when somebody else beat them to the punch I done this for them as sort of a consolation prize.

K E Y   T O   S P U R S

If the spur ain't here, it's not on the original

AMOUROUS AUTUMN | AND YOU THOUGHT YOUR TROUBLES WERE BEHIND YOU | A GOOD BRAND OF TRAILMIX | A RUDE AWAKENING | BACK NINE | BEAR NECESSITIES | BEES IN THE OUTHOUSE | BRAINWORMS | BROKE TO LEAD | BULLSEYE | CAFE OLÉ | CHICK MAGNET | CHINESE FIRE DRILL

COLD NOSE | CORRAL #9 | COWBOY TRAPPINGS | THE PRAIRIE BREEZE | THE GRASS IS ALWAYS GREENER | COWLISTHENICS | BOTTOMS UP! | CULTURE CLASH | DAISY | DANDELIONS FOR DAISY | DOES THIS HURT YET? | DUCK! | EVEN AT OUR AGE WE STILL GOT GREAT-LOOKING CALVES!

FIRST DAY OF THE MILENNIUM | GRATEFUL, AIN'T SHE? | HEARD YOU WAS LOOKING FOR A HAND | HE WAS JUST A HUNDRED YARDS FROM MARIANNE | HIGH ON THE HAWG | HUNG OUT TO DRY | ICE CAPADES | ICHABOD | IN YOUR DREAMS! | I SAID HEEL! | ITCHIN' FOR A BRITCHIN' | I TRAINED HIM MYSELF | JUST WHERE DO I START?

KID'S HORSE | LUCKY | LUNCH CREW | ONCE A YEAR | ONE CHEEK SNEAK | PREMEDITATED MANOUVRE | RAWHIDE | RETURN OF THE REDEYE | RIDIN' DRAG | RIDIN' THE RANGER | RODENTILE DELINQUENT | SALT LICK | SEVENTY-THREE SECONDS AND COUNTING

SITTIN' DOWN ON THE JOB | SUNFISHER | STRIKE FORCE | TAKING A TURN FOR THE NURSE | THAT SINKING FEELING | THERE'S ONE IN EVERY CROWD | TURNABOUT IS FAIR PLAY | TWO OLD GOATS | WATCHA DOIN' GRAMPA? | WHAT A STUPID-LOOKING HAT | WHO MOVED MY CAR? | WIDER GATES OR SMALLER COWS | ZELDA - QUEEN OF THE HERD